Brimming with creative inspiration, how-to projects, and useful information to enrich your everyday life, Quarto Knows is a favorite destination for those pursuing their interests and passions. Visit our site and dig deeper with our books into your area of interest: Quarto Creates, Quarto Cooks, Quarto Homes, Quarto Lives, Quarto Drives, Quarto Explores, Quarto Gifts, or Quarto Kids.

© 2018 Quarto Publishing Group USA Inc.

First Published in 2018 by Walter Foster Jr., an imprint of The Quarto Group.
6 Orchard Road, Suite 100, Lake Forest, CA 92630, USA.
T (949) 380-7510 F (949) 380-7575 www.QuartoKnows.com

Walter Foster Jr. titles are also available at discount for retail, wholesale, promotional, and bulk purchase. For details, contact the Special Sales Manager by email at specialsales@quarto.com or by mail at The Quarto Group, Attn: Special Sales Manager, 401 Second Avenue North, Suite 310, Minneapolis, MN 55401 USA.

ISBN: 978-1-63322-520-6

Digital edition published in 2018
eISBN: 978-1-63322-521-3

Written by Heidi Fiedler
Illustrated by Marta Sorte

Printed in China
10 9 8 7 6 5 4 3 2 1

50
WACKY THINGS
PETS DO

Weird & amazing things pets do!

Written by Heidi Fiedler
Illustrated by Marta Sorte

Walter Foster Jr.

TABLE OF CONTENTS

OUR WEIRD AND WONDERFUL FRIENDS

Millions of cats, dogs, rodents, birds, reptiles, and other beloved creatures share our homes. They curl up for cuddles, play games, and keep us company on adventures. For many people, life just wouldn't be as much fun without their furry friends.

Humans have been keeping pets for thousands of years. Our lives have changed a lot since the first pets joined our families, but animals behave the way they always have. We see dogs chasing their own tails, horses sleeping standing up, and cats kneading our legs. These behaviors may look pretty silly, but they make perfect sense in the wild. Since they can't talk, our pets can't explain why they do the odd things they do. But scientists are busy figuring it out!

Some of the animals in this book are more exotic than others, but all have been kept as pets and loved by humans. It doesn't matter if a pet is scaly or furry—or even if it has fangs. These animals love us and make us laugh with all their wacky ways.

NO. 1
FREE FALLIN'

Cats don't really have nine lives. They've just mastered the art of flipping in midair to land on their feet and survive falls from dramatic heights. Rather than panic when they enter free fall, kitties gain control and take advantage of physics. First they rotate the top half of their bodies and then fling their bottom halves in the opposite direction. The result is a stunning success rate with all four paws safe and sound on the ground!

MORE ABOUT CATS

Purring sounds peaceful, but cats also purr when they're at the vet or injured. So what is the real purpose of this noise? Cats purr by rapidly contracting and relaxing the muscles in their voice boxes. New studies suggest that purring vibrations might help strengthen their muscles and bones. Clever kitty!

NO. 2
POOP SOUP

Eating poop is normal. Totally normal. At least for man's best friend it is. Dogs are natural scavengers. They eat whatever they can find—including poop! Canines in the wild don't know where and when they'll eat next, so they eat whatever they can get. And that includes poop soup.

MORE ABOUT DOGS

Dogs rely on their sense of smell to understand the world. Their noses have about 4 times as many scent cells as cats and 14 times more than humans. That's why dogs are often used to find missing people.

NO. 3
DREAMLAND

Pass the pillow, please! Horses can doze standing up (although they do need to lie down for a deep sleep). Want to spot a standing horse snoozing? Look for a lowered head and drooping lips. Standing while they catch some shut eye allows horses to run from danger faster than if they were lying down. To make sure they don't fall down on the job, they lock the bones and ligaments in their legs into place. If you want to help your horse get a good night's sleep, keep the barn quiet and calm so it will feel safe enough to lie down.

MORE ABOUT HORSES

Horses make a lot of saliva. Adult horses can produce 35 to 40 liters a day! The amount varies depending on if they're eating dry hay or moist grass. But whatever they're eating, the saliva helps horses digest their food.

NO. 4
FREEZE!

Don't move a muscle! That's how reasonable rabbits respond to fear. They might look silly sitting frozen in the middle of the living room, but in the wild, this trick keeps them safe. Many predators attack whatever is moving, so if you're a rascally little rabbit who can stand as still as a statue until the threat passes, you just might escape becoming dinner. Hop on!

MORE ABOUT RABBITS

Excited rabbits race through the house, leap through the air, and kick their feet out. When they're simply happy, they'll flop down and roll onto their sides. Feel free to add your own sigh of contentment!

NO. 5
SSSLIP OF THE TONGUE

Flick! A forked tongue darts out. But what is it doing? It's not being used to tell *hiss*terical jokes. It's a *sss*ly sort of nose! What slithery snakes lack in the ability to see or hear, they make up for with their keen sense of smell. A single flick of the tongue can bring odors from the air into the snake's mouth, where the scent is detected. If the right side of the tongue has more food scent chemicals on it, the snake knows dinner is to the right. If the left side of the tongue detects the scent more strongly, the snake will slide on over to the left for a bite to eat. Pretty *sss*mart!

MORE ABOUT SNAKES
Just like people naturally prefer to use their right or left hand, snakes tend to move and coil in one direction over the other. Most choose clockwise rather than counterclockwise. Right on!

NO. 6
SNACK PACK

When a hungry hamster finds a snack, it stuffs its cheeks with food for later. First one nut, then another, then yet another—and maybe a little seed for the road too. Each nut is somehow crammed next to the last. How does it fit so much in there? The secret lies in those deep cheek pockets, which extend down to its hips like enormous pouches. They're the perfect accessory for a hungry hamster who always packs a snack!

MORE ABOUT HAMSTERS

Hamsters may appear cute and fluffy, but inside beats the wee heart of a warrior! They are dead serious about defending their territory. If another hamster gets too close, they will fight to the death. En garde!

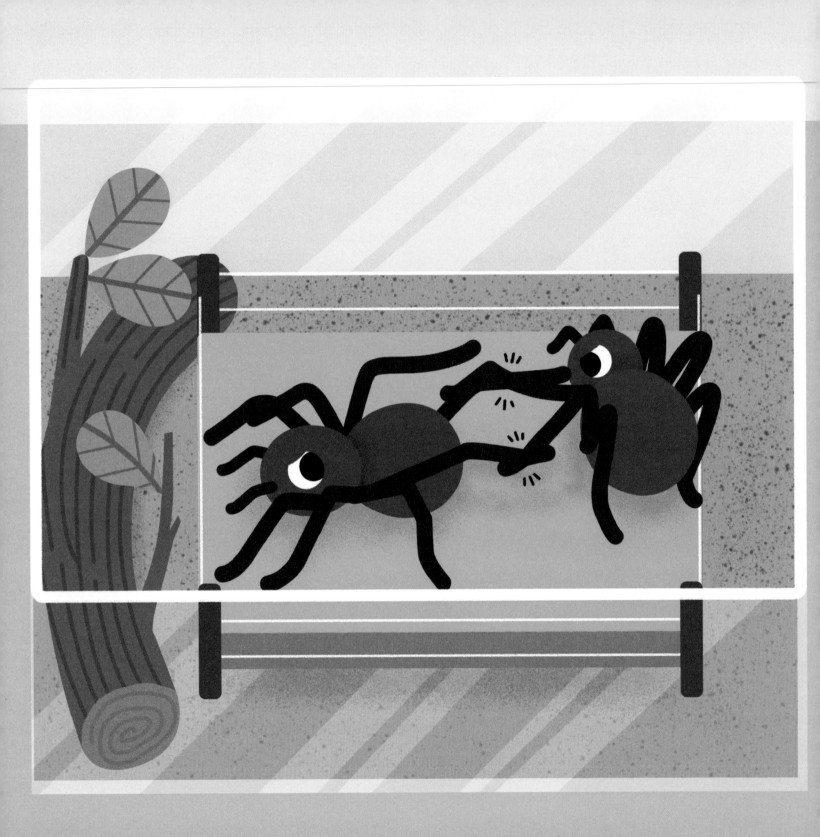

NO. 7
THROW DOWN

You don't have to be a vet to know tarantulas aren't the cuddliest of pets. They are the world's largest spiders, after all. They also aren't afraid to throw down if they're under attack. They bite and fling their sharp, bristly hairs at anyone who threatens them. These barbed hairs can cause quite an irritating rash. If your tarantula breaks it out, you know it can only mean one thing: back off!

MORE ABOUT TARANTULAS

There are more than 850 kinds of tarantulas. They all use venom to paralyze prey. The good news is that it's not harmful to humans. But it can sting!

NO. 8
SLIP AWAY

Whoops! There goes some fur. Oops! Lost a little more. When chinchillas feel threatened, they leave behind patches of hair. It helps these gentle creatures escape predators (or human hands that get too rough), but it can leave them exposed in more ways than one! And it takes fur up to six months to grow back. To prevent fur slip, smart chinchilla owners carefully hold their pet where the tail meets the body while supporting the legs until their furry friend relaxes enough to be held at the chest. And it doesn't hurt to talk sweetly to them either!

MORE ABOUT CHINCHILLAS

Chinchillas have very fine hair and oily skin, and it's easy for moisture to get caught in their fur. To stay clean in the wild, chins give themselves dust baths by rolling around in volcanic ash. Because most houses don't have volcanic ash just lying around, pet chins use a dust specifically made for them that can be purchased online or at pet stores.

NO. 9
FEEL THINGS OUT

Alert! Alert! Whiskers up! Rats use their whiskers to feel things—the same way people use their hands. They move their whiskers back and forth as they explore a new space. Even in the dark, whiskers help rats know where they are and what the space feels like. And if they're somewhere familiar, like a cozy cage, they can move extra fast by feeling for objects they might run into with their mustaches. Those are some wise whiskers!

MORE ABOUT RATS

Despite their reputation, rats are exceedingly clean animals. They are actually one of the cleanest pets you can own. They spend most of their time grooming themselves, which makes their fur super soft!

NO. 10
SCHOOL OF FISH

Goldfish aren't famous for being geniuses, but they're smarter than they look. With some schooling, they can do tricks, such as swimming through mazes, recognizing colors, and playing fetch. If you want to get serious about training your fish, you can teach them lessons—and give them straight A's—in everything from telling time to playing soccer. The class clown can even learn to swim through hoops!

MORE ABOUT GOLDFISH

Goldfish use teeth in their throats to crush their food. They don't have stomachs. Instead they break up food and absorb nutrients in their intestines.

NO. 11
TOAD À LA MODE

Lots of animals shed. Just ask any pet owner! But most don't eat what they leave behind. Toads aren't ones to waste a good meal though. They shed their skin, push it into their mouths, and eat it. A skin sandwich may not be your idea of a tasty treat, but toads make good use of the protein that's found in this slippery snack. And bonus: eating their skin ensures they won't leave a trail behind for predators who want to see them croak.

MORE ABOUT TOADS
It's a common myth that touching a toad can give you warts. While toads often have bumps on their skin, they don't actually give people warts! The small, rough bumps protect toads from predators.

NO. 12
SPIT BALLS

It's a big, bad world out there—at least when you're a wee little hedgehog. It pays to figure out what's what when you find something new in your neighborhood. That's why hedgehogs lick and bite the toys you place in their habitats. They use their mouths to explore unfamiliar objects. You might also see your hog work up a ball of spit and lick it onto its spines. This helps your hedgehog blend in with the toy's scent—just in case there's a big baddie approaching, and it needs to hide.

MORE ABOUT HEDGEHOGS

When hedgehogs get scared, they roll into a tight ball. And once those prickles are up, good luck holding your hog. Strong back muscles help them stay curled until they're good and ready to unroll.

NO. 13
WINK, WINK

Gerbils have tons of ways to talk to each other. How do they say hello in Gerbilese? Nose touches. A wink says they're happy or grateful. Gerbils that are curious stand up to get a better look—or sniff—at what's ahead. They leave their scent around the house by rubbing their bellies against everything as a way of saying, "That's mine." A loud squeak translates to "Danger! Danger!" And when everything is just right, you'll hear a gentle purr.

MORE ABOUT GERBILS
When gerbils need to warn others of danger, or show they like another gerbil, they stomp their back feet on the ground. When there's a group of gerbils, they thump together, forming a surprisingly loud but totally adorable drumline.

NO. 14
HAPPY DANCE

It's not your imagination—ferrets have moves! They break them out when they're super excited about a new toy or special food and have energy they can't use any other way. Fluffing their tails, leaping across furniture, and bouncing off the walls are all part of their happy dance. You can dance along with them. Just don't turn up the music too loud, or you'll miss the best part—the sound of ferret laughter!

MORE ABOUT FERRETS

Shiver me timbers! Ferrets are the pirates of the pet world. They steal and hide anything and everything they can find. Cell phones, jewelry, and keys are all favorite treasures to hoard. Argh! It's no coincidence the word *ferret* means "little thief" in Latin.

NO. 15
FAST FOOD

Baby seahorses get hungry like, well, horses. They don't have teeth or a stomach, so food passes through quickly, and they need to eat a lot to survive. That's why they gorge on so much food—up to 3,000 shrimp a day (brine shrimp, that is). Their long snouts let them cut through the water, so they can sneak up on prey again, again, and again...

MORE ABOUT SEAHORSES

Male seahorses give birth to thousands of baby seahorses at a time. Why so many? Less than 1 in 200 will survive. Once a brood is delivered, a male seahorse can get pregnant again later that same day, ready to start the process all over again!

NO. 16
TAIL TUSSLE

It's easy to forget our animal friends aren't human, until their wild instincts remind us. Mess with an iguana, and you'll see its long tail transform into a fierce weapon. These reptiles aren't afraid to use their long tails like a whip to strike whenever they feel threatened. And if a cat—or reckless human—makes a grab for an iguana, the tail will fall off to create a wiggly distraction, so the iguana can escape. Once the danger is over, iguanas can slowly regrow their tails.

MORE ABOUT IGUANAS

Iguanas are cold-blooded animals, which means their body temperatures change when the outside temperature changes. That's why they prefer warmer temperatures and often need a heat lamp in their enclosures!

NO. 17
ALL MINE

"This is mine! That's mine! And that is totally mine!"
If you've ever seen your rabbit rub its chin against its cage,
it's leaving a secret, if not subtle, message for other rabbits
to find. A gland under the chin releases a special scent.
Humans can't smell it, but the process leaves the rabbit's
signature scent on everything it touches. It's a rabbit's way
of marking its territory, which is (you guessed it!) just a
fancy way of saying "That's mine!"

MORE ABOUT RABBITS
Hippity-hop! Not sure where your rabbit
prefers to spend its time? Poop marks the
spot! Happy rabbits leave a trail of poop to
mark their territory.

NO. 18
SWEET SPOT

It's a peaceful but peculiar feeling to have a cat pawing at your leg. Cats often rhythmically push into something soft when they're being petted, but it can happen at other moments too. No one knows for sure why cats do it. Some think it's a leftover behavior from kittenhood, when young cats kneaded their mama's stomach to start her milk flowing. Others think it resembles the motion cats make when they want to create a smooth spot in the grass to lay on. Kneading may be a simple way to stretch their muscles, like a feline form of yoga. Or maybe it's just the way cats pet us!

MORE ABOUT CATS

Cats and their owners develop their own special code of meows and messages. But as much as our cats meow and yowl to get our attention, they don't meow at each other. Instead they're mostly silent when they're around other cats.

NO. 19
PIP POP

Have you ever been so excited you thought you might pop? Guinea pigs have! Of course, they don't actually pop (gross!), but they jump up and down like pieces of popcorn when they get to try a new food, meet a friend, or otherwise find themselves living the guinea pig good life. They also run around, kick their feet, and squeak. Boars, sows, and baby guinea pigs all do it. But the piglets pop the highest!

MORE ABOUT GUINEA PIGS
Prehistoric relatives of guinea pigs were enormous and rather terrifying. Three million years ago, they had foot-long front teeth and stood five feet tall. Definitely not pet material!

NO. 20
FASHIONISTAS

All animals pay attention to color. It helps them find food, stay safe, and choose a mate. And while lizards may be stone-faced, they're paying attention. One study even found they feel more relaxed with humans wearing certain colors of clothes. Can you guess what colors they prefer? It appears clothes the color of their own scales are most attractive, which is a bit like saying your favorite color is the color of your own eyes!

MORE ABOUT LIZARDS

When the short-horned lizard is attacked, first it tries inflating its body like a spiky balloon to ward off predators. If that doesn't work, the blood vessels around its eyes burst, and blood squirts out. The spray frightens dogs, wolves, and coyotes—and anyone else who's watching!

NO. 21
MOUSE HOUSE

In the wild, mice may live in garbage piles, but house mice are surprisingly neat. These nocturnal animals build complex burrows with long tunnels and always make sure they have an escape plan. And of course, they groom themselves several times a day, making sure they are in tip-top, tidy shape!

MORE ABOUT MICE
Mice use their nearly hairless tails for balance when climbing. Thin and nimble, their tails can grow as long as their bodies.

NO. 22
BUTTING HEADS

Wink, wink, nudge, nudge. Cats are subtle creatures—unless you're not getting the message. Then they aren't afraid to butt heads. But unlike rams or other more aggressive animals, cats rub their heads against us to show they like us. The behavior probably sounds familiar if you've ever tried to ignore a cat who wants to be petted. They'll use their foreheads and chins until you give them some of that sweet, sweet petting!

MORE ABOUT CATS

Why do cats weave between our legs and circle their tails around us when we come home? It's the cat version of a hug. Feral cats in the wild do the same thing. It's like saying, "I missed you!"

NO. 23
ROCK STAR

Do parrots prefer polka or punk? It may sound like a tongue twister, but it's actually a question your parrot can answer. Each parrot has its own musical preferences. Some like nothing more than to preen their feathers to Mozart. Others are happier whistling along to a zippy swing song. One study suggests that most parrots dislike techno music. It made them screech and squawk until it was turned off.

MORE ABOUT PARROTS
Parrots are some of the smartest creatures on Earth. Scientists are studying their ability to talk and count. They can even do addition and discuss math!

NO. 24
DOG PADDLE

Ducks aren't the only animals with webbed feet. Some dogs have paws that look more like flippers than feet. Labradors have extra large webbed paws that help them swim through water. Dachshunds use their webbed toes to dig through dirt when they're on the hunt. Redbone coonhounds wade through muddy swamps with their webbed feet. Whether they are swimming, digging, or hunting, these dogs deserve a belly rub!

MORE ABOUT DOGS

Veterinary eye doctors have found dogs can see shades of blue and yellow but not red and green. So to a dog, a bright orange ball on a green lawn appears as a dark yellow ball in light yellow grass. That's something to remember if your dog gives you a blank look while playing fetch!

NO. 25
FEARLESS FLYER

Your backyard might be too small to put their abilities to the test, but true to their name, sugar gliders can leap and then glide through the air for up to 55 yards (50 meters) in search of nectar, tree sap, and less sweet treats such as insects and seeds. The flaps of skin that connect the front arms to the back legs help them soar bravely through the trees, while their tails keep them steady. Given the chance, these pets often dine by moonlight and fly under the cover of night, because staying safe is always a sweet idea!

MORE ABOUT SUGAR GLIDERS

Sugar gliders do their best to fly right over trouble, but they haven't mastered the art of moving quietly. In fact these cute creatures are downright noisy. They bark, crab, hiss, and purr, depending on their mood.

NO. 26
SPF ZERO FUR

Is your hairless cat showing off its gorgeous wrinkles a little too much? Sphynx cats love sitting in warm patches of sunlight as much as other cats, but unlike most kitties, hairless cats can get sunburned. The good news is sunscreen will protect them. The bad news is Sphynx owners need to give their cats baths every week to wash off a greasy film that develops on their skin. And without any hair to keep dirt out of their ears, they need a good cleaning there too!

MORE ABOUT SPHYNX CATS

Despite their name, hairless cats aren't totally hairless. They actually have a layer of downy fuzz on their bodies (think suede jacket, not fluffy fur coat). Their skin comes in different colors, just like fur. And to make up for running around in their bare skin, they stay four degrees warmer than most cats.

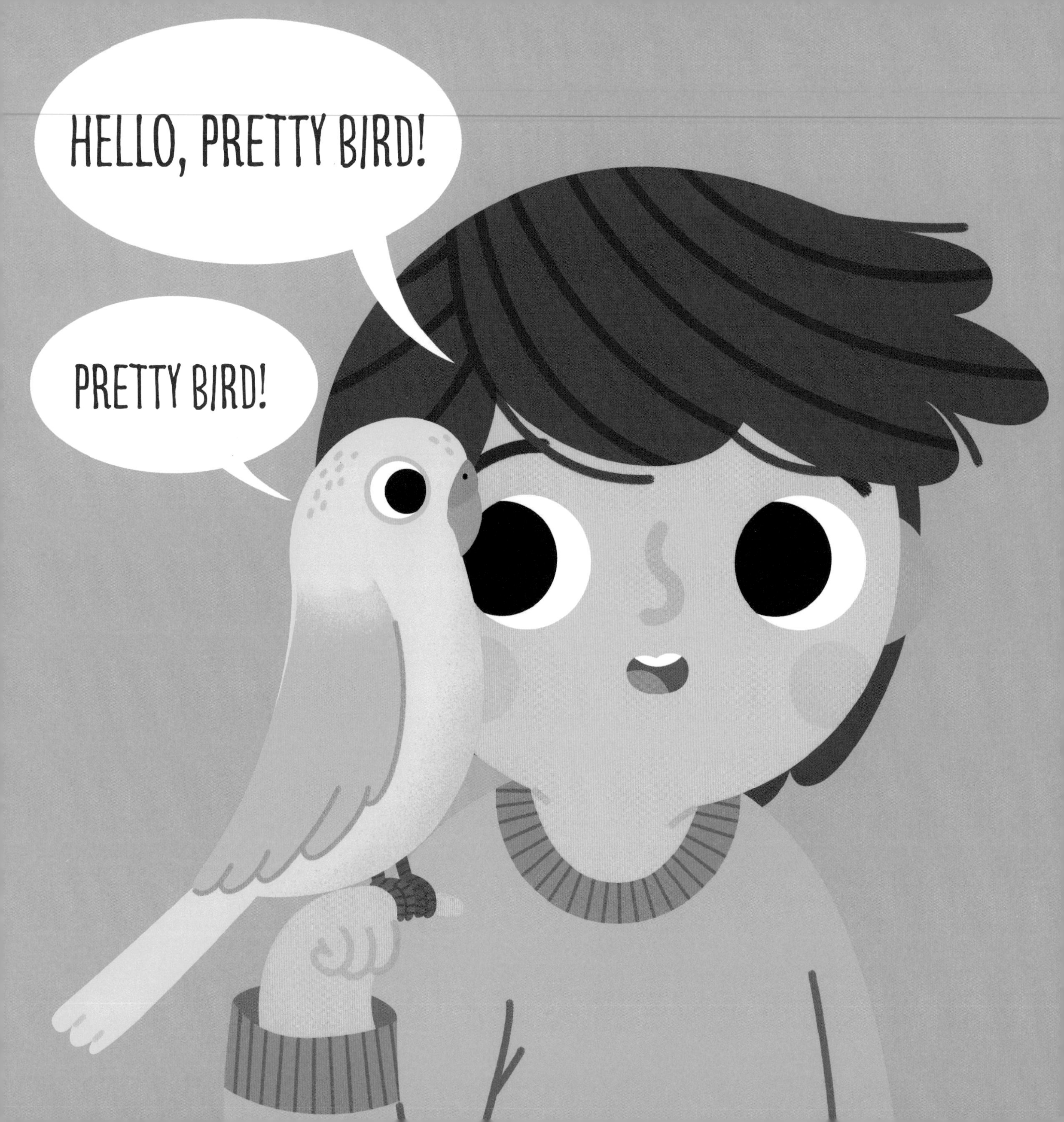
HELLO, PRETTY BIRD!
PRETTY BIRD!

NO. 27
CHIRP CHAT

Listen closely because your bird might be talking to you—or at least imitating you. Parakeets, and other birds that are able to mimic humans, always want to fit in, whether it's with your family or a flock of birds. They know if they don't chirp the right tune, they might get shut out of the local birdbath or left behind when the flock takes off. So if you're talking, they're talking.

MORE ABOUT PARAKEETS

Most of these social birds mate for life. If you're a parakeet owner, it's likely you'll find yourself with more than one, so they can keep each other company. They will also keep each other sleepy. Parakeet yawns are contagious, so when one lets a yawn fly, the others will soon follow, all the way to *zzzzz*leep!

NO. 28
BUG BITES

If you've ever wished you could fit just one more yummy bite into your belly, you might not be grossed out to learn frogs use their eyeballs to swallow food. How do they do it? When it's time to gobble down their meal, frogs squeeze their eyes closed and use their eyeballs to push food down their throats. The process helps them swallow their prey. Gulp!

MORE ABOUT FROGS

Frogs are really good jumpers. Their long legs act like springs to help push them forward—sometimes more than 20 times their length!

NO. 29
BIG BURPS

Turtles don't have vocal cords, but they can make some very vocal noises, including clucking sounds, high-pitched whines and hisses, and even belching sounds. These sounds are often involuntary, and are usually a result of fear. When turtles pull their head into their shell, they push air out of their lungs, which causes wacky sounds.

MORE ABOUT TURTLES

If you're thinking about adopting a turtle, it's wise to wonder what you might be doing in 100 years. Turtles can live a long time—even sometimes outliving their owners.

NO. 30
GOBBLE IT UP

You might wonder if your chicken lost its cock-a-doodle-do mind when you see it eating "food" like rocks, gold, or Styrofoam. But never fear! Chickens rely on an organ called a *gizzard* to digest their food, as questionable as it may be. As they nibble, they eat small pebbles. Inside the gizzard, the pebbles act like teeth, crushing whatever morsel the chicken has found. Yum?

MORE ABOUT CHICKENS

Catching a chicken is notoriously difficult. And it's no wonder—chickens can run up to 9 miles per hour!

MUD RUN

Pigs have a reputation for, well, living like pigs. They're happy to sleep in a sty and dig in the mud. But it's all for a good reason. The mud helps keep piggies cool. They aren't built for sweating, and those tubby bodies get hot easily. A good roll in the mud can lower their temperature at least three degrees as the water in the mud slowly evaporates. Mud also prevents sunburns and keeps insects off their sensitive skin. Plus a messy mud bath just feels good—try it!

MORE ABOUT PIGS

Sows (female pigs) like to live in groups with their piglets. Boars (male pigs) oink to their own drum, preferring to live on their own. Piglets form a power structure, where the top pigs eat first and bark at the lower pigs to back off.

NO. 32
MMM, CHEWY!

When we get hair in our mouths, we quickly spit it out. But a little hair never bothered a cat. In fact, cats spend hours rubbing, licking, and gently biting each other to show affection. Grooming family members helps cats keep the peace and remind each other who's in charge. If your cat chews your hair, take it as a compliment. It means your cat likes you better than most humans!

MORE ABOUT CATS

Cats often paw around their food bowl. The behavior is left over from wild ancestors who buried their food in the ground. Just like lions, your house cat wants to hide food from other animals. The pawing might not do any good indoors, but it means your cat is following its instincts.

NO. 33
WALK ON THE WILD SIDE

Does your chameleon look like it's walking across a tightrope, even when it's on solid ground? Your reptile isn't the only one who walks to a beat no one else can hear. All chameleons sway back and forth erratically when they walk. The process might look like the chameleon is still learning to walk, but it's totally normal. Scientists aren't sure why they do it. Some think it's to help them blend in with the swaying trees they climb in, but no one has proved it yet.

MORE ABOUT CHAMELEONS

How do chameleons climb on branches and vines so easily? Their feet work the same way salad tongs do. By pinching and clamping, they can make their way through the trees—or the tops of their tanks.

NO. 34
OOEY GOOEY NEST

If your betta fish's tank looks a little slimy, it might be mating season. Male bettas build nests by blowing bubbles of mucus. They gulp air from the surface and spit out bubbles coated in mucus. The process takes hours. And when the nest of bubbles is complete, the male's work still isn't done. He has to fight off any females that might try to eat the eggs the nest is meant to protect.

MORE ABOUT BETTA FISH

In the wild, betta fish are generally shades of brown and gray. Pet bettas are so vibrant because they've been bred to be bright reds, greens, and blues.

NO. 35
BARK ATTACK

Does your dog go bonkers in front of the mirror? Barking at mirrors may look bizarre to humans, but it makes lots of sense to dogs. Smell is the most important sense for our canine friends, and that dog in the mirror doesn't smell like anything at all. So even though it looks, moves, and sounds like a dog, without a scent to track, your dog may as well have seen a ghost. And that's enough to make anyone howl.

MORE ABOUT DOGS

Puppies haven't learned how to communicate with humans yet, so it's up to us to understand what they're saying. A grunt means your pup is pleased. Lip licks may mean your pup is nervous. Blinking means your dog is thinking hard—about what is another question!

NO. 36
AWKWARD ANGLE

If you've ever watched your gecko tiptoe across the top of its tank, you know these reptiles are master climbers. They can race up walls and hang upside down. Try following that, predators! What's their secret? Hairy toes! The bottom of each toe is covered in millions of tiny hairs. And if they need to quickly de-stick? They just stretch their toes.

MORE ABOUT GECKOS

Here's some "tail talk." Geckos wiggle their tails to signal a variety of moods. They let other geckos know they're near and excited with a quick shake. A slow wave is likely a distraction so predators will attack the gecko's tail and not its body.

NO. 37
HAHA-LARIOUS

Want to know a secret? Rats may repulse some people, but they're in for a sweet surprise. These rodents love to be tickled, and if you're lucky, you'll even hear them laugh. The ultrasonic squeaks are too high for most people to hear, but slow them down, and they sound like pure joy!

MORE ABOUT RATS

Rat teeth never stop growing. Rats spend lots of time gnawing on whatever they can find. That includes everything from plastic to tinfoil, and even concrete! It sounds brutal, but the constant gnawing actually helps rats keep their teeth from getting too long.

NO. 38
BRING HOME A GIFT

Although it may not seem like it, cats are being anything but rude when they place a fresh kill at our feet. Swatting a bird to death doesn't have anything to do with whether your kitty is getting enough kibble. So what's up with all the gross gifts? Cats bring us dead animals because they think us poor house-bound humans don't know how to hunt. And the truth is, they're probably right. Meow!

MORE ABOUT CATS

Cats make great pets, but their office skills aren't so hot. Just as you're about to tap out a brilliant new idea on your computer, your feline friend curls up in a ball right where you're working. Cats love to sleep on our laptops because they're warm. It might not hurt that they get to be close to us too.

NO. 39
TURTLE LOVE

"My, what red ears you have!" "Are you trying to get my claws afluttering?" That's hot talk for red-eared slider turtles. While they may not actually talk, their courtship dance does include fluttering their claws at each other. And some turtles even use their claws to stroke their beloved's face.

MORE ABOUT TURTLES

When they get hungry, wild North American wood turtles stomp for worms. The process involves raising their shells, standing tall, and then dropping down to the ground. Boom! The worms surface, and the turtles can feast without going to the trouble of digging.

NO. 40
GO, GO, GUPPY!

Belly flops are no fun, especially when there's no water to catch you! So why do guppies jump out of their tanks so often? The short answer is they're curious, and they want to find what else is out there. It's just one more behavior that doesn't make sense at home, but makes a lot of sense out in the wild, where fish benefit from traveling to see if the next pond over is safer or more interesting.

MORE ABOUT GUPPIES

Most fish lay eggs, but guppies give birth to live young. You can even see them inside their mother before they're born. Just be sure to put some plants in your tank, so the young will be able to hide from their parents once they are born. Grown guppies have been known to eat their young!

NO. 41
SIP SLIDIN'

Salamanders don't just breathe through their skin.
They can drink through it too. No need for a straw!
If your slinky friend is starting to look parched, spray a
bit of spring water on the ground covering in its cage.
It will absorb the water it needs through its skin.
And whatever you do, don't dress up your salamander.
These pets do best naked!

MORE ABOUT SALAMANDERS

Like most reptiles and amphibians, salamanders
prefer not to be handled by humans. These
fascinating creatures have delicate skin, so loving
owners should to avoid petting them.

NO. 42
WILD WINDS

You might love feeling the wind in your hair, but for horses it's a wake-up call. Despite their size, in the wild, horses are prey. They've evolved to be on the lookout for threats. But it's not the wind they're afraid of. Horses get spooked when it's windy because it can block out sounds they need to hear. Even worse, it carries unfamiliar smells and makes the grass, leaves, and bushes move, which could be the first sign of a predator lurking. That's why a little wind in the mane doesn't feel so good to horses.

MORE ABOUT HORSES

Clip, clop! Horses have four types of gaits, or ways of moving: walk, trot, canter, and gallop. Each has a different rhythm and speed. Experienced riders can tell the difference just by listening to the beat!

NO. 43
TAIL SPIN

'Round and 'round they go! Where they'll stop, no one knows—not even those crazy dogs chasing their own tails. What's behind their wild whirls? Dogs chase their own tails when they have a bad itch or just want to play. Some puppies don't understand their tails are attached to them! But try to avoid laughing. That can encourage the whirling. Sometimes tail chasing can get a little too intense, or it can be a sign that your dog is stressed. Woof!

MORE ABOUT DOGS

If you hear a loud snort coming from your dog, you might think it's choking on something, but it might just be reverse sneezing. It's as weird as it sounds and is common in dogs. It's often caused by the same thing that causes normal sneezes: dust!

NO. 44
LOOK BOTH WAYS

Is your chameleon giving you the eye? If the answer is no, look again. It might be giving you the other eye. Chameleon eyes can move independently, so they can look in two different directions at once. Up, down, and left to right, it's like eyeball ping-pong. But wherever they're looking, these eyes are focused on finding food.

MORE ABOUT CHAMELEONS
Chameleons are famous for changing colors. Some changes reflect body temperature. Other times, the colors communicate what chameleons are feeling, much like the clothes we choose to wear.

NO. 45
WHISTLE A HAPPY TUNE

If your cockatiel whistles at you, be proud. These cuddly birds tend to whistle at their favorite people, toys, and birds—including their own reflection in the mirror! Want to teach your cockatiel to sing songs? Show them how it's done. Then play the song on repeat. When your bird starts whistling the melody, give it a treat. Just be sure to choose a song you'll want to hear every day for the rest of your life!

MORE ABOUT BIRDS

When people grind their teeth, it usually means they're tense. But birds grind their beaks when they're happy. They also use their beaks to wrestle and play with other birds.

NO. 46
RUN AROUND

Mice spend lots of time running on the wheels in their cages. They crave exercise, especially at night, and these long runs to nowhere keep mice in good shape. They also love climbing on all sorts of things, so be sure to include ropes, ladders, and blocks in the cage. And if you want to leave your mice a special treat, install a hammock, so they can kick up their feet after a long run.

MORE ABOUT MICE

Life can be pretty squeaky in the mouse house. Male mice break out into song to impress female mice. Sadly, the squeaks are too high-pitched for humans to hear, so any duets with your furry friend are out of the question.

NO. 47
ORANGE OVERLOAD

Rabbits are known for chowing down on carrots. Owners like to give carrots as a treat, but they shouldn't do it too often. (Rabbits should really be eating grass, hay, and leafy greens like spinach.) Rabbits don't eat carrots in the wild. Some go a little crazy when they eat too many. Some rabbits even get cavities from eating too many carrots, which are more like candy than vegetables for them. So be careful with carrots— no one wants to visit the bunny dentist!

MORE ABOUT RABBITS

What's up with those big long teeth? Rabbits have four large, sharp front teeth. They act like scissors, cutting and breaking down plants. Smaller teeth in the cheeks grind the food before swallowing. Because rabbits use them so much, their teeth never stop growing.

NO. 48

WALK LIKE AN EGYPTIAN

Would you walk your ferret on a leash? King Tut and Cleopatra may have! Some Ancient Egyptian tombs are said to have pictures of animals that look very much like ferrets being walked on leashes. If that's true, it means ferrets were among the first pets in ancient civilizations. Historians think they were prized for keeping rats and mice out of grain storage.

MORE ABOUT FERRETS

Ferrets have been friends with some famous folks over the years. Queen Elizabeth I had a portrait painted with her ferret, and Leonardo da Vinci, the famous artist, frequently portrayed ermines, which are ferret relatives.

NO. 49
SWAP MEET

Despite their name, hermit crabs are surprisingly social and prefer to hang out with other crabs. In fact, if you keep several crabs together, they'll throw shell-swapping parties! The practice lets them find the perfect shell as they grow bigger. The shells protect their soft bellies, so finding the right home is important. And when one crab makes a switch, it starts a chain reaction. The others know a new shell will open up—and it just might be a shell worthy of a shindig!

MORE ABOUT HERMIT CRABS

Hermit crabs don't like to eat the same meal twice in a row. They prefer a beachy buffet. A little fish, some seaweed, and even a bite of apple will satisfy these crustaceans—just not for two meals in a row!

NO. 50
MUTT BUTT

Sniffing butts may not be how you want to greet your BFF, but that's just how dogs do it! Dogs learn about other dogs by smelling their backsides. It's sort of like the canine equivalent of a handshake. A single whiff lets doggie friends know a dog's gender, health, diet, and mood. With all that information, it's more like reading a friend's diary than an invisible handshake.

MORE ABOUT DOGS

Just like humans, dogs dream when they sleep. Experiments suggest they dream about dog things like running and hunting. And smaller dogs have shorter dreams than bigger dogs!

Also in this series

50 Wacky Things Animals Do
describes 50 peculiar animal behaviors that seem too crazy to be true—but are!

50 Wacky Things Humans Do
describes 50 wild and unbelievable things the human body is able to do.

50 Wacky Inventions Throughout History
describes 50 weird, silly, and mind-boggling inventions.